Hail Mary,
Mystical Rose,
Tower of David,
Tower of Ivory,
House of Gold,
Ark of the Covenant,
Gate of Heaven,
Morning star,
Health of the sick,
Refuge of sinners,
Comforter of the afflicted,
Help of Christians,
Queen of angels,
Queen of patriarchs,
Queen of prophets,
Queen of martyrs,
Queen of confessors,
Queen of virgins,
Queen of all saints.

— *The Litany of Loreto*

MARY

WRITTEN AND ILLUSTRATED

BY

DEMI

MARGARET K. McELDERRY BOOKS
NEW YORK   LONDON   TORONTO   SYDNEY

Margaret K. McElderry Books An imprint of Simon & Schuster Children's Publishing Division
1230 Avenue of the Americas, New York, New York 10020 Copyright © 2006 by Demi

Book design by Michael Nelson The text for this book is set in Minister.
The illustrations for this book are rendered in paint and ink. Title calligraphy by Jeanyee Wong Manufactured in China
2 4 6 8 10 9 7 5 3 1
LIBRARY OF CONGRESS CATALOGING-IN-PUBLICATION DATA Mary / compiled and illustrated by Demi.
p. cm. ISBN-13: 978-0-689-87692-9 ISBN-10: 0-689-87692-0 1. Mary, Blessed Virgin, Saint—Biography—
Quotations—Juvenile literature. I. Demi. II. Title. BT605.3.M37 2006   232.91—dc22   2005005844

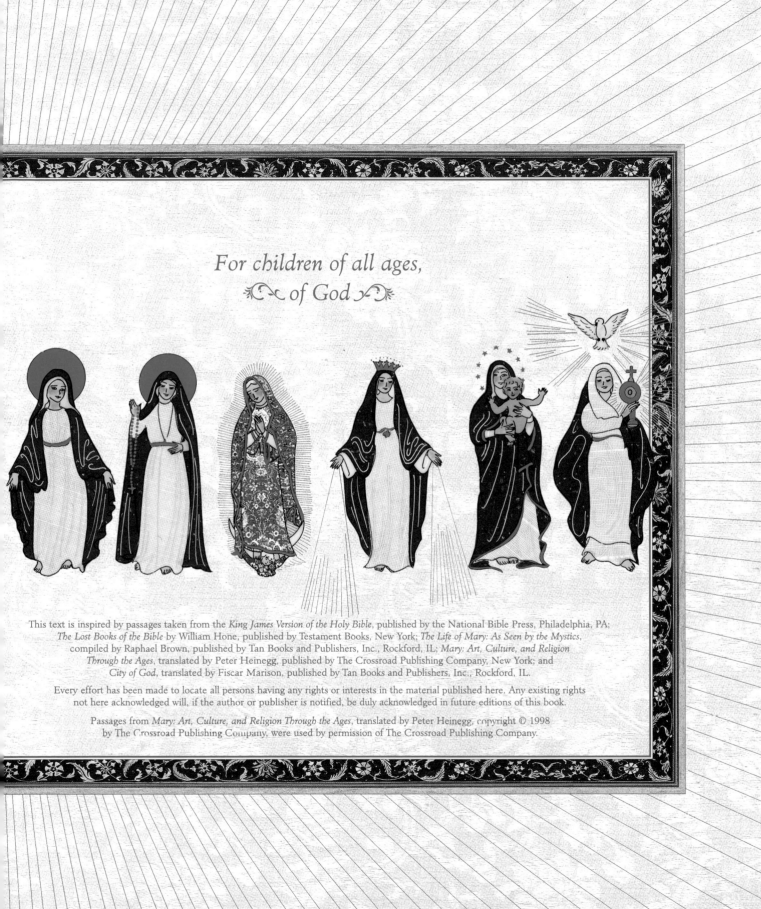

For children of all ages,
~ of God ~

This text is inspired by passages taken from the *King James Version of the Holy Bible*, published by the National Bible Press, Philadelphia, PA; *The Lost Books of the Bible* by William Hone, published by Testament Books, New York; *The Life of Mary: As Seen by the Mystics*, compiled by Raphael Brown, published by Tan Books and Publishers, Inc., Rockford, IL; *Mary: Art, Culture, and Religion Through the Ages*, translated by Peter Heinegg, published by The Crossroad Publishing Company, New York; and *City of God*, translated by Fiscar Marison, published by Tan Books and Publishers, Inc., Rockford, IL.

Every effort has been made to locate all persons having any rights or interests in the material published here. Any existing rights not here acknowledged will, if the author or publisher is notified, be duly acknowledged in future editions of this book.

Passages from *Mary: Art, Culture, and Religion Through the Ages*, translated by Peter Heinegg, copyright © 1998 by The Crossroad Publishing Company, were used by permission of The Crossroad Publishing Company.

The Family of Mary

THE BLESSED AND EVER GLORIOUS Virgin Mary, sprung from the royal race and family of David, was born in the city of Nazareth, and educated at Jerusalem, in the temple of the Lord.

Her father's name was Joachim, and her mother's Anna. The family of her father was of Galilee and the city of Nazareth. The family of her mother was of Bethlehem.

THE LOST BOOKS OF THE BIBLE,
THE BOOK OF MARY, CHAP. 1:1–2

They lived for about twenty years . . . in the favor of God, and the esteem of men, without any children.

But they vowed if God should favor them with any issue, they would devote it to the service of the Lord; on which account they went at every feast in the year to the temple of the Lord.

THE BOOK OF MARY, CHAP. 1:5–6

Joachim Prays for Mary

When [Joachim] had been there for some time, on a certain day when he was alone, the angel of the Lord stood by him with a prodigious light.

Be not afraid, Joachim, nor troubled at the sight of me, for I am an angel of the Lord sent by him to you, that I might inform you, that your prayers are heard, and your alms ascended in the sight of God.

THE BOOK OF MARY, CHAP. 2:1, 3

. . . Anna your wife shall bring you a daughter, and you shall call her name Mary; She shall, according to your vow, be devoted to the Lord from her infancy, and be filled with the Holy Ghost from her mother's womb; She shall neither eat nor drink anything which is unclean, nor shall her conversation be without among the common people, but in the temple of the Lord; that so she may not fall under any slander or suspicion of what is bad.

THE BOOK OF MARY, CHAP. 2:9–11

So in the process of her years, as she shall be in a miraculous manner born of one that was barren, so she shall, while yet a virgin, in a way unparalleled, bring forth the Son of the most High God, who shall, be called Jesus, and, according to the signification of his name, be the Savior of all nations.

THE BOOK OF MARY, CHAP. 2:9–12

She shall be, immediately upon her birth, full of the grace of the Lord, and shall continue during the three years of her weaning in her father's house, and afterwards, being devoted to the service of the Lord, shall not depart from the temple, till she arrives to years of discretion.

THE BOOK OF MARY, CHAP. 3:3

THE BIRTH OF MARY

So Anna conceived, and brought forth a daughter, and according to the angel's command, the parents did call her name Mary.

THE BOOK OF MARY, CHAP. 3:11

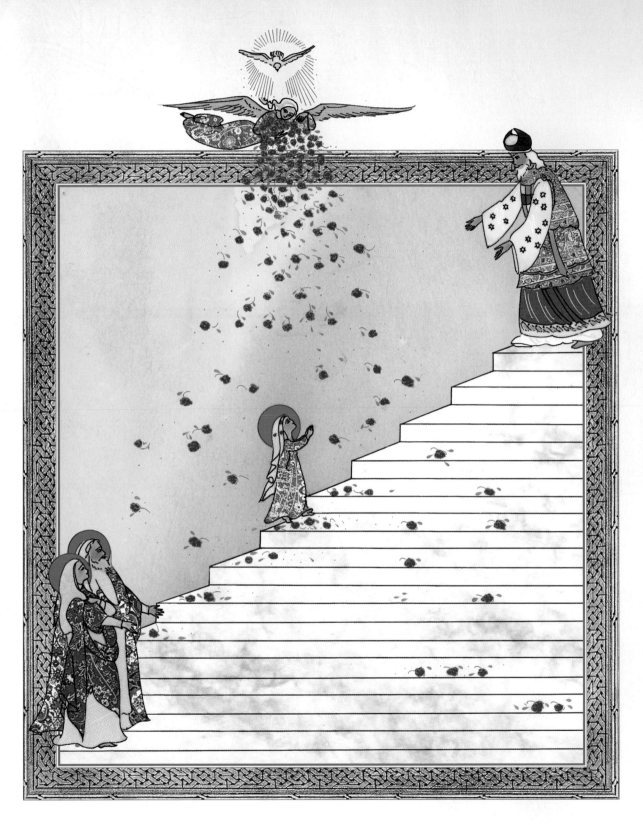

THE MIRACLE ON THE TEMPLE STAIRS

And when three years were expired, and the time of her weaning complete, they brought the Virgin to the temple of the Lord with offerings. And there were about the temple . . . fifteen stairs to ascend. The parents of the blessed Virgin and infant Mary put her upon one of these stairs; . . . The Virgin of the Lord . . . went up all the stairs one after another, without the help of any to lead or lift her, that any one would have judged from hence that she was of perfect age.

Thus the Lord did, in the infancy of his Virgin, work this extraordinary work, and evidence by this miracle how great she was like to be hereafter.

THE BOOK OF MARY, CHAP. 4:1–2, 4, 6–7

MARY TO MARRY

But the Virgin of the Lord, as she advanced in years, increased also in perfections, and . . . the Lord took care of her. For she every day had the conversation of angels, and every day received visitors from God, which preserved her from all sorts of evil, and caused her to abound with all good things; So that when at length she arrived to her fourteenth year . . . all good persons, who were acquainted with her, admired her life and conversation.

At that time the high-priest made a public order. That all the virgins who . . . were come to this age, should . . . be married. To which command . . . Mary the Virgin of the Lord alone answered, that she could not comply with it.

THE BOOK OF MARY, CHAP. 5:1–5

JOSEPH, THE HUSBAND OF MARY

The high-priest . . . went to consult God. And immediately there was a voice from the ark . . . that it must be inquired or sought out by a prophecy of Isaiah to whom the Virgin should be given and be betrothed; For Isaiah saith, there shall come forth a rod out of the stem of Jesse, and a flower shall spring out of its root, And the Spirit of the Lord shall rest upon him, the Spirit of Wisdom and Understanding, the Spirit of Counsel and Might, the Spirit of Knowledge and Piety, and the Spirit of the fear of the Lord shall fill him.

Then, according to this prophecy, he appointed, that all the men of the house and family of David, who were marriageable, and not married, should bring their several rods to the altar, And out of whatsoever person's rod after it was brought, a flower should bud forth, and on the top of it the Spirit of the Lord should sit in the appearance of a dove, he should be the man to whom the Virgin should be given and be betrothed.

THE BOOK OF MARY, CHAP. 5:12–17

Among the rest there was a man named Joseph, of the house and family of David, and a person very far advanced in years . . .

When he did bring his rod, and a dove coming from Heaven pitched upon the top of it, everyone plainly saw, that the Virgin was to be betrothed to him.

THE BOOK OF MARY, CHAP. 6:1, 5

THE ANNUNCIATION

And . . . the angel Gabriel was sent from God unto a city of Galilee, named Nazareth, To a virgin espoused to a man whose name was Joseph, of the house of David; and the virgin's name was Mary.

And the angel came in unto her, and said, Hail, thou that art highly favored, the Lord is with thee: blessed art thou among women. And when she saw him, she was troubled at his saying, and cast in her mind what manner of salutation this should be.

And the angel said unto her, Fear not, Mary: for thou hast found favor with God. And, behold, thou shalt conceive in thy womb, and bring forth a son, and shalt call his name JESUS. He shall be great, and shall be called the Son of the Highest: and the Lord God shall give unto him the throne of his father David: And he shall reign over the house of Jacob for ever; and of his kingdom there shall be no end.

Then said Mary unto the angel, How shall this be, seeing I know not a man?

And the angel answered and said unto her, The Holy Ghost shall come upon thee, and the power of the Highest shall overshadow thee: therefore also that holy thing which shall be born of thee shall be called the Son of God. . . .

And Mary said, Behold the handmaid of the Lord; be it unto me according to thy word. And the angel departed from her.

LUKE 1:26–35, 38

THE VISITATION

And Mary arose in those days, and went into the hill country with haste, into a city of Juda; And entered into the house of Zacharías, and saluted Elisabeth. And it came to pass, that, when Elisabeth heard the salutation of Mary, the babe leaped in her womb; and Elisabeth was filled with the Holy Ghost: And she spake out with a loud voice, and said, Blessed art thou among women, and blessed is the fruit of thy womb.

LUKE 1:39–42

THE MAGNIFICAT

And Mary said, My soul doth magnify
the Lord, And my spirit hath rejoiced in
God my Savior. For he hath regarded
the low estate of his handmaiden: for,
behold, from henceforth all generations
shall call me blessed. For he that is
might hath done to me great things; and
holy is his name.

And his mercy is on them that fear
him from generation to generation. He
hath shewed strength with his arm; he
hath scattered the proud in the imagina-
tion of their hearts. He hath put down
the mighty from their seats, and exalted
them of low degree.

He hath filled the hungry with good things; and the rich he hath sent empty away. He hath holpen his servant Israel, in remembrance of his mercy; As he spake to our fathers, to Abraham, and to his seed for ever.

LUKE 1:46–55

THE BIRTH OF JESUS

And it came to pass in those days, that there went out a decree from Caesar Augustus, that all the world should be taxed.

And Joseph also went up from Galilee, out of the city of Nazareth, into Judea, unto the city of David, which is called Bethlehem; (because he was of the house and lineage of David:) To be taxed with Mary his espoused wife, being great with child.

And she brought forth her firstborn son, and wrapped him in swaddling clothes, and laid him in a manger; because there was no room for them in the inn.

And there were in the same country shepherds abiding in the field, keeping watch over their flock by night. And, lo, the angel of the Lord came upon them, and the glory of the Lord shone round about them: and they were sore afraid.

And the angel said unto them, Fear not: for, behold, I bring you good tidings of great joy, which shall be to all people. For unto you is born this day in the city of David a Savior, which is Christ the Lord.

LUKE 2:1, 3–5, 7–11

The Presentation of Jesus in the Temple

And when the days of her purification according to the law of Moses were accomplished, they brought him . . . to present him to the Lord.

And, behold, there was a man . . . whose name was Simeon; and the same man was just and devout . . . and the Holy Ghost was upon him. And it was revealed unto him by the Holy Ghost, that he should not see death, before he had seen the Lord's Christ.

And he came by the Spirit into the temple: and when the parents brought in the child Jesus . . . Then took he him up in his arms, and blessed God, and said, Lord, now lettest thou thy servant depart in peace, according to thy word: For mine eyes have seen thy salvation, Which thou hast prepared before the face of all people; A light to lighten the Gentiles, and the glory of thy people Israel.

And Joseph and his mother marvelled at those things which were spoken of him. And Simeon blessed them, and said unto Mary his mother, Behold, this child is set for the fall and rising again of many in Israel; and for a sign which shall be spoken against; (Yea, a sword shall pierce through thy own soul also,) that the thoughts of many hearts may be revealed.

LUKE 2:22, 24–35

THE WISE MEN WORSHIP

Now when Jesus was born in Bethlehem of Judea in the days of Herod the king, behold, there came wise men from the east to Jerusalem, Saying, Where is he that is born King of the Jews? for we have seen his star in the east, and are come to worship him.

When Herod the king had heard these things, he was troubled. . . . And when he had gathered all the chief priests and scribes of the people together, he demanded of them where Christ should be born. And they said unto him, In Bethlehem of Judea: for thus it is written by the prophet.

Then Herod, when he had privily called the wise men, enquired of them . . . what time the star appeared. And he sent them to Bethlehem, and said, Go and search diligently for the young child; and when ye have found him, bring me word again, that I may come and worship him also.

When they had heard the king, they departed; and, lo, the star, which they saw in the east, went before them, till it came and stood over where the young child was. When they saw the star, they rejoiced with exceeding great joy. And when they were come into the house, they saw the young child with Mary his mother, and fell down, and worshipped him: and when they had opened their treasures, they presented unto him gifts; gold, frankincense, and myrrh. And being warned of God in a dream that they should not return to Herod, they departed into their own country another way.

MATTHEW 2:1–12

THE FLIGHT INTO EGYPT

And when they were departed, behold, the angel of the Lord appeareth to Joseph in a dream, saying, Arise, and take the young child and his mother, and flee into Egypt, and be thou there until I bring thee word: for Herod will seek the young child to destroy him.

When he arose, he took the young child and his mother by night, and departed into Egypt: And was there until the death of Herod: that it might be fulfilled which was spoken of the Lord by the prophet, saying, Out of Egypt have I called my son.

MATTHEW 2:13–15

JESUS TEACHES IN THE TEMPLE

And the child grew, and waxed strong in spirit, filled with wisdom: and the grace of God was upon him.

Now his parents went to Jerusalem every year at the feast of the passover. And when he was twelve years old, they went up to Jerusalem after the custom of the feast. And when they had fulfilled the days, as they returned, the child Jesus tarried behind in Jerusalem; and Joseph and his mother knew not of it. But they, supposing him to have been in the company, went a day's journey; and they sought him among their kinsfolk and acquaintance. And when they found him not, they turned back again to Jerusalem, seeking him.

And it came to pass, that after three days they found him in the temple, sitting in the midst of the doctors, both hearing them, and asking them questions.

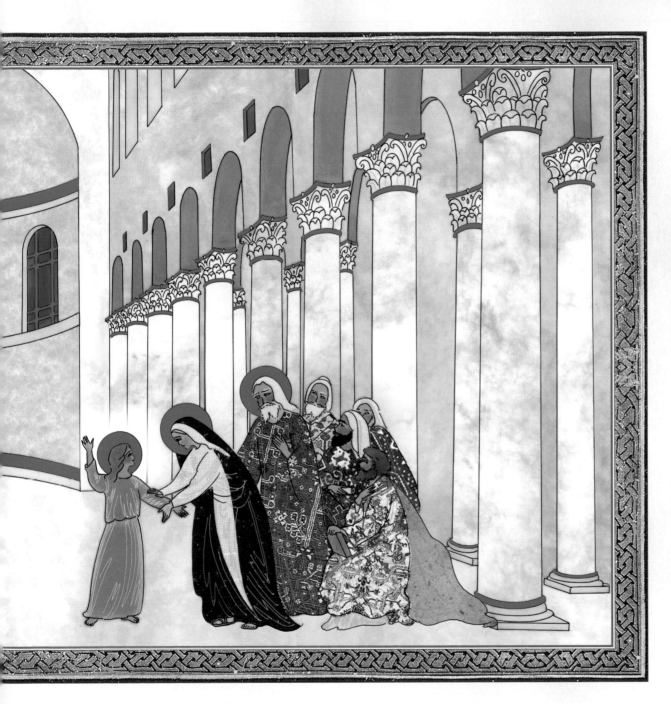

And all that heard him were aston-
ished at his understanding and answers.
And when they saw him, they were
amazed: and his mother said unto him,
Son, why hast thou thus dealt with us?
behold, thy father and I have sought
thee sorrowing.

And he said unto them, **How is it
that ye sought me? wist ye not that I
must be about my Father's business?**

LUKE 2:40–49

**Who is my mother, or my brethren? And
he looked round about on them which
sat about him, and said, Behold my
mother and my brethren! For whosoever
shall do the will of God, the same is my
brother, and my sister, and mother.**

MARK 3:33–35

And they understood not the saying
which he spake unto them. And he went
down with them, and came to Nazareth,
and was subject unto them: but his
mother kept all these sayings in her heart.

LUKE 2:50–51

THE MARRIAGE FEAST AT CANA

And the third day there was a marriage in Cana of Galilee; and the mother of Jesus was there: And both Jesus was called, and his disciples, to the marriage. And when they wanted wine, the mother of Jesus saith unto him, They have no wine.

Jesus saith unto her, Woman, what have I to do with thee? mine hour is not yet come.

His mother saith unto the servants, Whatsoever he saith unto you, do it.

And there were set six waterpots of stone . . . Jesus saith unto them, Fill the waterpots with water. And they filled them up to the brim. And he saith unto them, Draw out now, and bear unto the governor of the feast. And they bare it.

When the ruler of the feast had tasted the water that was made wine, and knew not whence it was: (but the servants which drew the water knew;) . . . This beginning of miracles did Jesus in Cana of Galilee, and manifested forth his glory; and his disciples believed on him.

JOHN 2:1–11

THE MINISTRY OF MARY

Jesus spent much time teaching his mother all that she must know and do later for his church. . . . He taught her the meaning and value of the Sacraments and dogmas of the church, and he described to her the whole history of his church until the end of the world, together with all its saints and martyrs and doctors and prelates. He also showed her how to apply this knowledge in a practical way to her daily life, so that she might be well prepared to serve him and His Mystical Body the Church as Divine Providence planned.

Once when Mary was almost overcome at the thought of the future ingratitude of men toward their Savior, Jesus ordered the angels to console her by singing canticles of praise to God for her.

Then Christ gave his mother a still deeper understanding of the mystery of sin and redemption, and he encouraged her by revealing to her the great number of the predestined apostles and saints of the church.

The Lord also showed his mother how he was going to conduct his preaching and how she was to cooperate with him and help him to found his church.

The Life of Mary: As Seen by the Mystics

THE POWER OF PRAYER

Accompanied by Mary, Jesus visited the sick and the grief-stricken, especially among the poor. He restored health of body to many, and assisted the dying, giving them true peace of mind. . . . Often while nursing sick women and children with her own hands, Mary prayed to Jesus to cure them—and he gave her the power to do so.

Thus she secretly healed many persons, restoring sight to the blind and even bringing the dead back to life, yet in such a hidden way that all the glory was attributed to her Son, in whose name she performed these miracles.

In order to keep informed of the doings of our Savior the most blessed Mary needed no other assistance than her continual visions and revelations. [She] spent nearly all her time in prayer . . . interceding for sinners by her prayers and mortifications.

The rest of the time she conversed with her holy angels, whom the Lord had commanded to attend her in visible form. They kept her informed of all her Son's actions and prayers, so she was able to pray with him when he prayed, in the same posture and with the same words.

[With] rigorous fasting, in all his prayers and exercises, his prostrations and genuflections, she followed our Savior, not omitting any of them.

THE LIFE OF MARY: AS SEEN BY THE MYSTICS

THE SACRIFICE OF MARY

One day . . . Mary heard a voice of marvelous power say to her: "Mary, my daughter . . . offer your Son to me as a sacrifice."

Realizing the time had at last come for the redemption of mankind through the Public Life and Death of Christ, she replied generously: "Eternal King and Almighty God, Lord of all, he is thine and so am I. What then can I offer thee that is not more thine than mine? Yet because he is the life of my soul and the soul of my life, to yield him into the hands of his enemies at the cost of his life is a great sacrifice. However, let not my will but thine be done. I offer up my Son in order that he may pay the debt contracted by the children of Adam."

The Blessed Trinity immediately rewarded and consoled her by a vision in which she was shown the glory and the good that would result from Jesus' sacrifice and hers. When she came out of this rapture, Mary was prepared to endure the pain of being separated from her beloved Son and Lord.

THE LIFE OF MARY: AS SEEN BY THE MYSTICS

THE CRUCIFIXION

Now there stood by the cross of Jesus his mother, and his mother's sister, Mary the wife of Cléophas, and Mary Magdalene.

When Jesus therefore saw his mother, and the disciple standing by, whom he loved, he saith unto his mother, **Woman, behold thy son!** Then saith he to the disciple, **Behold thy mother!** And from that hour that disciple took her unto his own home.

After this, Jesus knowing that all things were now accomplished, that the scripture might be fulfilled, saith, I thirst. Now there was set a vessel full of vinegar: and they filled a sponge with vinegar, and put it upon hyssop, and put it to his mouth.

When Jesus therefore had received the vinegar, he said, It is finished: and he bowed his head, and gave up the ghost.

JOHN 19:25–30

MARY: MOTHER OF THE CHURCH

Then returned they unto Jerusalem from the mount called Olivet, which is from Jerusalem a sabbath day's journey. And when they were come in, they went up into an upper room, where abode both Peter, and James, and John, and Andrew, Philip, and Thomas, Bartholomew, and Matthew, James the son of Alpheus, and Simon Zelotes, and Judas the brother of James. These all continued with one accord in prayer and supplication, with the women, and Mary the mother of Jesus, and with his brethren.

ACTS 1:12–14

A few days before the Ascension, the Holy Trinity said to [Mary] as she was meditating in a corner of her room: "Beloved, ascend higher! . . . My daughter, I entrust and consign to you the church founded by my only-begotten Son, the new Law of Grace which he has established in the world, and the people which he has redeemed."

And the Holy Spirit announced: ". . . I communicate to you my wisdom, and in your heart shall be deposited the mysteries and teachings and all that the Incarnate Word has accomplished in the world."

And the Son said to her: "My beloved Mother, I go to my Father, and I leave you in my stead."

Then the Holy Trinity declared to the throng of adoring angels and saints: "This is the Protectress of the Church and the Intercessor of the faithful. In her are contained all the mysteries of our Omnipotence for the salvation of mankind. Whoever shall call upon her from his heart and obtain her intercession, shall secure for himself eternal life. What she asks of us shall be granted."

. . . And from that day she was endowed with the spiritual care of the church, the Mystical Body of her divine Son, and became the loving Mother of all its children, until the end of the world.

THE LIFE OF MARY: AS SEEN BY THE MYSTICS

PENTECOST

Early on Pentecost . . . a luminous silvery cloud descended from Heaven, and . . . an enormous mass of light seemed to condense and become transparent, like a sun throwing out its flames in all directions.

Suddenly the sound of a violent wind arose, as though a cyclone were approaching from above, and the air resounded with a tremendous roaring . . . This . . . gave way to a display of light, a soft murmur, and a warm, healing breeze. From out of the cloud appeared rays which intercrossed seven times in a fiery rainbow and fell like burning drops . . .

[Everything] was flooded with a dazzling light. The Apostles and especially the Blessed Virgin seemed to be blazing with a mystical transparent luminosity. . . . Then into each mouth there fell a jet of fire, . . . in which the Holy Spirit came to them, filling each person with divine inspiration and grace and wisdom.

THE LIFE OF MARY: AS SEEN BY THE MYSTICS

. . . And [they] began to speak with other tongues, as the Spirit gave them utterance.

ACTS 2:4

In the holy Mother of God these effects were altogether supernatural. She was utterly transformed and exalted in God. . . . By this wonderful blessing the [Apostles] were transformed into truly apostolic founders and missionaries of the Church of Christ.

THE LIFE OF MARY: AS SEEN BY THE MYSTICS

ANNOUNCEMENT OF MARY'S DEATH

From this hour on the most blessed Mother of God remained, for as long as she lived, entrusted to the special care of John.

PSEUDO-MELITO

In the twenty-second year after Jesus had conquered death and gone to heaven, Mary spent one day in a remote corner of her house, enflamed by the wish to see the Redeemer again . . .

[Behold,] an angel appeared to her in gleaming light, greeted her, and said, "I greet you, blessed by the Lord; receive the greeting of him who offered Jacob his greeting through the prophets; behold, I bring you a palm branch from God's Paradise; let it be carried before your coffin, when in three days you will be transported to heaven in your body. For your Son awaits you with the thrones and with the angels and with all the powers of Heaven."

PSEUDO-MELITO

Mary's Death

Then Mary said to the angel: "I pray you, let all the apostles of my Lord Jesus Christ gather around me."

The angel answered her: "All the apostles will be brought here today through the power of Jesus Christ."

They entered the house and greeted her . . . She said: "The Lord has brought you here to comfort me. . . . I beg you all to watch unceasingly with me until the hour when the Lord appears and I shall leave this body."

And behold, all at once the Lord Jesus appeared with a great band of angels in shining glory, and the angels sang hymns of praise to the Lord. And the Lord spoke: "Come, you chosen one, most precious pearl, enter into the dwelling of eternal life."

Then Mary . . . prayed to the Lord . . . "Receive your maidservant, O Lord, and redeem me from the power of darkness. . . ."

The Savior replied, ". . . Come then in peace, for the heavenly hosts await you, so that I may lead you into the joys of Paradise."

And when the Lord had spoken these words, the Virgin arose, stretched out on her bed and gave up the ghost, thanking God. Then the apostles saw such a burst of glory that no human tongue can describe, for it surpassed the whiteness of snow and the brightness of silver.

Pseudo-Melito

THE ASSUMPTION OF MARY

Then the Lord kissed her and handed her over to his angels, to take her to Paradise . . . After these words the Lord went up into heaven on a cloud; but the angels accompanied him and bore the most blessed Mary, the Mother of God, into God's Paradise.

PSEUDO-MELITO

THE CORONATION OF MARY

Now Jesus said to the blessed Virgin, "See now the glory to which you have been exalted." She looked up and saw greater glory than the human eye can bear. And behold, Enoch, Elijah, Moses and all the prophets and patriarchs and the elect came and adored the Lord and blessed Mary. . . . And the Lord made the sun stop before the gates of heaven. . . . The Lord sat above the sun in a chariot of light. And Mary saw the great gate of Jerusalem and rejoiced!

PSEUDO-MELITO

Hail Mary,
Mystical Rose,
Tower of David,
Tower of Ivory,
House of Gold,
Ark of the Covenant,
Gate of Heaven,
Morning star,
Health of the sick,
Refuge of sinners,
Comforter of the afflicted,
Help of Christians,
Queen of angels,
Queen of patriarchs,
Queen of prophets,
Queen of martyrs,
Queen of confessors,
Queen of virgins,
Queen of all saints.

— *The Litany of Loreto*